Scottie Pippen: The Inspiring Story of One of Basketball's Greatest Small Forwards

An Unauthorized Biography

Table of Contents

Foreword

As impactful as Michael Jordan was for the Chicago Bulls, none of the accomplishments by the Bulls would have been possible without Jordan's incredible supporting cast. Scottie Pippen was not just a supporting cast member of the legendary Chicago Bulls, but also a star of his own, providing the Bulls with a secondary scoring option whenever teams might draw a double team on Jordan. Scottie was Robin and Michael was Batman; yet one without the other would have made it much more difficult to have won so many NBA Championships. Scottie was and remains one of the most versatile players to ever grace the basketball court both offensively and defensively. On offense, he could direct an offense like a point guard and rebound like a power forward; on defense, he could completely shut down the perimeter. Thank you for downloading *Scottie Pippen: The Inspiring Story of One of Basketball's Greatest Small Forwards.* In this unauthorized biography, we will learn Scottie Pippen's incredible life story and impact on the game of basketball. Hope you enjoy and if you do, please do not forget to leave a review!

Cheers,

Clayton Geoffreys

Introduction

Tom and Jerry. Lone Ranger and Tonto. Sherlock Holmes and Dr. Watson. Batman and Robin. Jordan and Pippen. It's hard to describe a man who many have believed was a mere sidekick to Michael Jordan. However, like Jerry, Tonto, Dr. Watson, and Robin, Scottie Pippen also established a name for himself in the game of basketball. Most of his career happened in the shadows of Jordan and people fail to realize that without Pippen, Chicago potentially would not have created the wining Bulls dynasty. Pippen once said, "Sometimes a player's greatest challenge is coming to grips with his role on the team." He not only came to grips with his role, but embraced it, quietly racking up impressive statistics while giving his teammates the spotlight. The 6-time NBA Champion and all-leader in steals and assists among forwards, is one of the most versatile players in NBA history. Although Pippen averaged over 20 points a game along with 7 rebounds, he was continually overshadowed by the shooting guard god, Jordan. It wasn't until Pippen was charged with guarding Magic Johnson in the 1991 NBA Finals that everyone began to take notice and see Pippen in his own right. The world soon began to uncover the mystery surrounding Pippen's rise to fame in the basketball world.

In the height of his prime, Pippen made 10 consecutive All-NBA First Defensive teams, and was only one of three NBA players to record 200 steals and 100 blocks in a single season. He was known to block the lanes of opposing teams with his unusually long wingspan (2.2m) and jumping ability. Coach Phil Jackson once described him as a "one man wrecking crew." His tireless work ethic and selfless playing style often resulted in him leading the Bulls in blocks and assists. He finished 23rd in all-time assists in his career. Pippen is truly one of the league's greatest treasures and few players in NBA history have actually matched his versatility. He was an incredibly unique player. On defense, he combined his height with strength and athleticism and there was no area he didn't excel in. He was also a versatile, lock-down defender capable of guarding several positions such as: small forward, shooting guard and point guard. During his era and possibly beyond, he is arguably the best perimeter and wing defender to have ever existed. When he was forced to defend the low block, he succeeded there too. He was truly a defensive masterpiece, outfitted with all the tools necessary to become an elite player.

As amazing as Pippen was on the defensive end, many argue that he was even more versatile on offense. Listed as a small forward, yet having the body of a smaller power forward, Pippen possessed it all. He could score off the dribble. He was a good cutter and opponents struggled to defend him because he size was no match against other point guards. He was a decent outside shooter, 32% from downtown, and an above average free throw shooter. So peeking out from under Jordan's shadow, Pippen will be remembered as one of the most versatile and agile players of all times, influencing the next generation of NBA players.

Chapter 1: Childhood and High School Years

September 25th, 1965, was probably much like any other day in the small town of Hamburg, Arkansas. However, for Ashley and Ethel Pippen, it was the day their 12th and final child was born. They named their baby boy, Scottie Maurice Pippen. Hamburg was a relatively small town and there weren't many activities for Pippen at the time so he bonded with his siblings by playing basketball.

Entering high school, Pippen was an athlete determined to succeed. He played both football and basketball, but eventually turned his focus towards basketball. As a senior, Pippen stood at just 6 feet and weighed150 pounds. While Pippen did manage to lead his team to the state finals, and earned himself a place with All-Conference team honors, he still didn't receive a scholarship to any college.

Hence, Pippen began his basketball career in the shadows. He didn't necessarily excel in academics, and only got into college after his coach called in a favor to the University of Central Arkansas, an NAIA school.

Chapter 2: College Years at the University of Central Arkansas

Pippen's basketball career was almost over before it ever began because he couldn't get into college. However, as a favor to Pippen's high school coach, the University of Central Arkansas offered him a job as a student manager. He received financial aid for being the team manager and also worked summers as a welder to supplement his finances. In addition to working a part time job in a factory, he signed as a walk-on player for the college team. He managed to earn a spot and a scholarship during his sophomore season. As the team's manager, he was responsible for trivial tasks such as getting water or replacing towels. However, something amazing started to happen as he grew older; Pippen transformed into an athletic beast, similar to Lebron James. He eventually emerged as the team's undisputed best player, averaging 23 points, 10.1 rebounds, and 4.3 assists as a senior. Throughout his college career, he managed to collect numerous accolades and conference titles in both his junior and senior years, and was voted twice onto the NAIA All-Conference team. Even though he grew experience and skills over four years in college, Pippen was scared that his team's lack of post-season performances would hinder his chances into making the NBA. It wasn't until Pippen was invited to the Portsmouth College All-Star event that his stock value as a draft-pick skyrocketed. At the event, he completely demolished the competition and managed to attract the notice of the Chicago Bulls. His incredible muscular frame and massive wingspan made him a stand out in that year's NBA draft.

Chapter 3: Scottie's NBA Career

Early Career (1987-1990)

Pippen was selected as the 5th overall pick, by the Seattle Supersonics, and coming from a pretty small and average NAIA college, this was quite a feat. Sill, at the time, Pippen was a relatively unproven rookie and Olden Polynice was a center capable of defending the inside and protecting the rim. Furthermore, the Chicago Bulls General Manager Jerry Krause saw Pippen play and began to wonder if he could pair him up with someone else, a player named Michael Jordan. Fearing that Pippen was already on someone else's radar, he quickly made a trade to the Seattle Supersonics who held that year's 5th overall pick. As a result, a deal was reached which immediately traded Pippen to Chicago, but little did anyone know, Pippen would find his place in Chicago and go on to become a 6-time NBA Champion and perennial all-star. Playing alongside Michael Jordan forced him to step up his game and allowed him to quickly develop his skills as a player.

No one knew it then, but today, it is clear who benefitted from this trade. Krause set into motion a turn of events that would change NBA history for a decade with this duet.

Pippen made his NBA debut against the Philadelphia 76ers and there began his long and prosperous career. He posted 10 points, 2 steals, 4 assists, and 1 rebound; just showing a glimpse of what was to come. With fellow Bulls player, Jordan, as a leader and motivator, Pippen slowly refined his skills and developed new ones. The teammates would often play games of one-on-one. These friendly games lasted several hours because both men had such drive and were top players of their generation. Pippen first began the postseason as a reserve like during the regular season, but he soon replaced Sellers in the starting line up in the fifth and final game of a first-round series against the Cleveland

Cavaliers. Pippen contributed with 24 points, 6 rebounds, and 3 steals for the Bulls' 107-101 victory. Then, Coach Doug Collins decided to keep him in a starting role for the next round. Unfortunately though, Chicago lost to their bitter rivals, the Detroit Pistons, in five games of the Eastern Conference semi-finals.

Still, helping the Jordan-led bulls to their first conference semi-finals in years was a victory in itself. Each year, Pippen developed more and more; eventually emerging as a perennial all-star. During his sophomore year as a Bull, Pippen began to show the variety of skills that would eventually make him a superstar and constant triple-double threat. Pippen remained the "sixth man" in his first 16 appearances, but started all but one game thereafter. For the season, he averaged a total of 14.4 points, 6.1 rebounds and 3.5 assists per game. In the game against the Los Angeles Clippers, Pippen began what would eventually become the norm for him, recording the first of 20 career regular season triple-double games, with 15 points, 12 assists and 10 rebounds. Being recognized as a premier forward throughout the league, he earned his first all-star credits during the 1990 game with career high numbers in all categories. Nevertheless, the Detroit Pistons "Bad Boys" continually foiled any plan of an NBA Championship until their breakthrough in the 1990-1991 season.

First in the 3 Peat

Finally, Chicago had exorcised its play-off demons and soon cast their own spell, beating its long-time nemesis, the Detroit Pistons, with an unequivocal four-game sweep in the Eastern Conference finals. Historically, teams experienced the Finals at least once before actually winning the title. Facing an experienced opponent like Magic Johnson and the Los Angeles Lakers, many believed the Bulls were not capable of pulling off the impossible, but a funny thing happened on the way to the Forum. Despite losing Game 1 at home in the final seconds, Chicago defied the odds and bounced back to win Game 2 by 21 points. Pippen's 32 points led the Bulls in the decisive Game 5, silencing all of the doubters with his skills in scoring. Pippen proved that he was not just Jordan's sidekick; he was also capable of taking over a game by himself. Pippen took the 1991 postseason as an opportunity to prove to the world that the Chicago Bulls were not a one-man gang. Without a doubt, Jordan carried the Bulls to their first-ever NBA Championship, but Pippen was equally responsible. He consistently contributed, averaging 21.6 points, 8.9 rebounds, 5.8 assists, and 2.47 steals per game during all 17 play-off games.

The next season, a new powerhouse arose in the west, the Portland Trail Blazers. Their superstar player, Clyde Drexler, was hyped up to be the new match for Jordan. Sports Illustrated even named him as Jordan's "Number One Rival." Much like Magic was the previous year, the match-up was incredibly exciting. The Chicago Bulls led by Jordan and Pippen stormed the league to an overall record of 67-15. In the Western Conference, Portland won the Pacific Division once again and thoroughly destroyed each team they encountered in the playoffs. To the media, it was to be an epic battle between a few of the greatest superstars of that era. While the series MVP was obviously Michael Jordan, Pippen still managed to stand out during each game. Becoming a distributor, he earned the most assists every game, proving that he was an incredibly versatile player. Pippen averaged numbers beyond other players in the league at 19.5 points, 8.3 rebounds, and 4.6 assists. By now, he had established himself as one of the NBA's elite players. In 1991-92, he appeared in his second NBA All-Star Game. He was initially selected as a reserve, but eventually started in place of the injured Larry Bird, and at the end of the season he landed on the All-NBA Second Team and NBA All-Defensive First Team, which was a first for him.

The following season was much different, since both Pippen and Jordan played on the Dream Team at the Olympics. Although the US won the Olympic gold, the games had taken a toll on the two superstars, as they were exhausted and weak when they returned to camp. This was thought to have had a tremendous effect on their play throughout the season, as they only won 57 games that year. The team realized that in order to be successful, their two superstars would need time to recover. Despite all this, the Bulls got off to a surprisingly hot start in the post-season, sweeping both the Atlanta Hawks and the Cleveland Cavaliers. Beating a surprisingly resilient Knicks team, the Bulls then managed to beat the Phoenix Suns four games to two. At this point, people made the argument that Pippen was not a true star; he was only being carried by Jordan and without him the Bulls would not be anything. A sudden turn of events would change all that as Jordan decided to retire following the death of his father that year. Pippen found himself holding the reins of the team, and positioned to prove himself. Carefully examining his play-off statistics, this seemed like a job for which Pippen had already prepared himself. Pippen racked up minutes on the court, averaging 41.5 minutes per game in the postseason, thus helping the Bulls to their third straight NBA title, a feat that had not been done since the Boston Celtics in the mid-1960s. He also had his best series in the Eastern Conference finals against the Knicks, averaging 22.5 points and 6.7 rebounds while shooting .510 from the floor.

Years without Jordan

With Jordan's unexpected retirement after the 1993–94 season, a new leader emerged from Jordan's shadow. That leader was Scottie Pippen. He earned All-Star Game MVP honors that year and led the Bulls in all the major statistical categories, scoring, assists, and blocks. He was also second in the NBA in steals per game, averaging 22.0 points, 8.7 rebounds, 5.6 assists,

2.9 steals, and 0.8 blocks per game, while shooting 49.1% from the field and a career-best 32% from the 3-point line. You name it, and Pippen could do it. He earned the first of three straight All-NBA First Team selections, and finished third in MVP voting that year. The Bulls finished the season with 55 wins, only two fewer than the year before. They silenced any doubter who thought a Bulls team, sans Jordan, would falter under pressure without their superstar.

However, an uncharacteristic play for Pippen happened during his first year without Jordan against the New York Knicks. During the 1994 NBA Playoffs, the Eastern Conference semi-finals had matched the Bulls against the New York Knicks. The Bulls had destroyed them en route to a three-peat each of their previous seasons beforehand. On May 13, 1994, down 2–0 in the series in a pivotal Game 3, Bulls coach Phil Jackson needed someone from his team to step up if they were to have any chance of going on to the conference finals. With only 1.8 seconds remaining on the clock and the score tied at 102; Jackson surprisingly designed the last play for the European rookie Toni Kukoc, with Pippen being instructed to inbound the basketball. Pippen, who had been the superstar and undisputed leader in Jordan's absence, became so enraged at Jackson's decision to not let him take the potential game-winner that he refused to leave the bench after the timeout. This shocked everyone because Pippen was always known to be a team player. Teammate Steve Kerr remarked, "I don't know what got into Pippen. He's such a great teammate and maybe the pressure was getting to him and he just could not take it anymore, no one knows for sure but he is a team player." Realizing that Jackson trusted a rookie over an experienced veteran such as himself was an insult. His coach couldn't muster the trust to let him take the winning shot, and Pippen didn't like it.

Nevertheless, Pippen redeemed himself during Game 6 of that same series where he made one of the most signature plays of his career. Midway through the third quarter, Pippen caught the ball during a Bulls fast break play, and charged towards the basket, as another future hall of famer, Patrick Ewing, jumped up to challenge the shot. Having fully extended the ball, Pippen absorbed body contact and a foul from Ewing. This counted as an and-one and he dunked the ball, in spite of Ewing's hand in his face. Pippen landed several feet away from the basket along the baseline, and ended up standing over a fallen Ewing.

Uncharacteristically, Pippen then began taunting both Ewing and then Spike Lee, who was known for sitting courtside supporting the Knicks, and received a technical foul. This then extended the Bulls' lead to 17 points, which they won 93–79. Though this series saw an exciting seven games, Pippen and the Bulls could not compete with the Knicks and lost the 1994 Eastern Conference semi-finals. Many thought the loss was foreshadowed in the final seconds of Game 5. Pippen was called by referee Hue Hollins for a questionable foul on Knicks' Hubert Davis, which allowed the Knicks to shoot the game-winning free throws. This helped lead the Knicks to a seven-game series victory. This series is worth noting because all seven games of the series were won by the home team. The Knicks earned home-court advantage and they walked away with the series win.

As with the conclusion of any season, rumors of trade involving Pippen swirled during the 1994 off-season. Many believed the Bull's General Manager was looking to trade Pippen in exchange for another all-star forward, Shawn Kemp. However, the trade was never made as it was announced that Michael Jordan would be returning to the Bulls late in that 1994-1995 season. While the Pippen-led Bulls did not do nearly as well in the current season as they had in the season before, for the first time in years the Bulls were in danger of missing the playoffs. Why they were not doing well could be attributed to many factors, including Horace Grant's departure in free agency. This left a void in interior defense and rebounding. The Bulls were just 34–31 prior to Jordan's return for the final 17 games, yet Jordan led them to a 13–4 record to close out the regular season. Even with Jordan's return, Pippen finished the 1994-1995 season leading the Bulls in every major statistical category; points, rebounds, assists, steals, and blocks and while doing so, becoming only the second player in NBA history to accomplish this feat (Dave Cowens did it in 1977-1978; and since then it has been achieved also by Kevin Garnett in 2002-2003 and LeBron James in 2008-2009). Pippen was then rewarded with an All-Star berth and selection to both the All-NBA First Team and the NBA All-Defensive First Team that year due to his superb season. With Jordan returning, the Bulls managed to finish the regular season at 47-35 to claim third place in the Central Division. The Bulls dominated and finished the first round of the play-offs series with the Charlotte Hornets before you could say, "Charlotte Hornets." However, the Orlando Magic was too much to handle at the time and the Bulls were defeated in the conference semi-final.

Second in Three-Peat

During the offseason, there were several notable additions to the Bulls; the most significant was two-time NBA champion Dennis Rodman. With his rebounding and interior defense, the Bulls posted the best regular-season record in NBA history (72–10) in 1995-1996. This was a year of redemption for the Bulls, who were determined to prove that they were the best team in the NBA, and seemed to put forth even more dedication. They had a 72 win season right before the playoffs, and demolished each and every team they encountered, with their final opponent being the Seattle Supersonics. Winning the series in 6 games, Pippen's role was significant with his wing defense and offensive facilitation. It earned him an All-NBA First Team defense award, and it was clear that Pippen was an incredibly important member of that team. Later that year, Pippen became the first person ever to win an NBA championship and then an Olympic gold medal in the same year twice, playing for Team USA at the 1996 Atlanta Olympics.

Coming back from their 4th NBA Championship in six years and a record breaking 72–10 season, the Chicago Bulls seemed to have reached all of their goals. Head Coach Jackson then wanted to relieve the team of some pressure and therefore began practicing for the upcoming season slowly to give his team more time to recover. Still, it did not take long for all the talent on the team to heat up because even with a much more relaxed training camp, the Bulls started the season with a blistering 17–1 start and had the league's best record of 42–6 entering the all-star break. Celebrating the league's 50th Anniversary, both Pippen and Jordan were each selected as one of the NBA's 50 Greatest Players of all time. The ceremony was held at halftime of the 1997 NBA All-Star Game which took place on

February 9, 1997. Phil Jackson, then the Chicago Bulls head coach, was honored as one of the 10 greatest coaches in NBA history. The 1992 Chicago Bulls Championship team and the 1996 Chicago Bulls Championship team, of which Pippen had pivotal roles, were selected as two of the greatest teams in NBA history. In the All-Star game itself, Pippen went 4–9 from the field, finishing with 8 points as well as 3 rebounds and 2 assists in just 25 minutes of play. During the season, Pippen scored a career high of 47 points in a 134–123 win over the Denver Nuggets on February 18. He was 19–27 from the field, and in addition, grabbed 4 rebounds, dished out 5 assists and had 2 steals in 41 minutes of play. On February 23, Pippen was voted "Player of The Week" for his efforts. This would be his 5th time to receive that award, yet it was also his last. As the league entered its final weeks in preparation for the playoffs, the Bulls suffered some serious setbacks. Bill Wellington had a ruptured tendon in his left foot. Dennis Rodman had injured his knee. Toni Kukoc had injured his right foot. Still, the Bulls went on to win their 5th championship, but this put even more pressure on Pippen and Jordan to fill the gaps caused by the injuries. Even with all of these unfortunate injuries, Chicago finished a league-best 69–13 record. Their chances for having back-to-back 70-win season, which would have been a new record, floated just out of reach when Pippen missed a game-winning 3-pointer. Regardless, for his defensive capabilities in the 1996-1997 season, Pippen once again earned an NBA All-Defensive First Team honors for the 7th consecutive year received All-NBA Second Team honors.

Fighting through an injury to his foot in the Eastern Conference finals, against the Miami Heat, Pippen helped the Bulls scrape by an 84–82 victory over the Utah Jazz in game 1 of the NBA Finals. Pippen then scored 27 points while Jordan scored 31. With the Bulls trailing by one point in the 4th quarter, they secured an 81–79 lead after Pippen managed to barely block Antoine Carr, and then made his third 3-pointer with only 1:11 remaining on the clock. Refusing to lose, John Stockton answered with a 3-pointer of his own with 51.7 seconds left to give Utah an 82–81 lead. Jordan was fouled with only a minute remaining and he made only 1 of 2 free throws with 35.8 seconds left to tie it at 82. Then, Karl Malone was fouled by Rodman with only 9.2 seconds left and had a chance to give Utah the lead. Later, it was revealed that Pippen psyched him out, saying that, "Just remember, the mailman doesn't deliver on Sundays, Karl," right before Malone stepped up to the line. Out of character for Malone, he missed both free throws. Jordan then got the rebound and quickly called a timeout with 7.5 seconds remaining. With the game on the line, the Bulls decided for Jordan to take the final shot. He dribbled out most of the waning seconds, and then launched a 20-foot shot that went in right at the buzzer to give Chicago a 1–0 series lead. Game 2, the opposite occurred, Pippen and Jordan dominated the Jazz completely, and comfortably defeated the Jazz by 12 points. The Jazz managed to respond back, and with the Bulls struggling in game 3, they were defeated. Although Pippen did tie a then finals record of seven 3-pointers, the Bulls still lost 104–93 without it even being a close contest. After losing the next game, the Bulls won game 5, Pippen finished with 17 points, 10 rebounds and 1 steal in 45 minutes. This game will probably forever be known as the infamous, "Flu Game," because after securing a Chicago win, the weakened Jordan collapsed into Pippen's arms, creating an iconic image and symbolizing the guts and sportsmanship that go into a win.

During Game 6 of the 1997 NBA Finals, Pippen made a play showing why he was one of the 50 greatest players of all time. Trailing by only two points, the Jazz looked for a final shot to stay alive, but Pippen knocked away Bryon Russell's inbound pass with a quick steal and rolled the ball over to Toni Kukoc, who easily finished with a dunk to seal the championship. Pippen then finished the game with 23 points, 9 rebounds, 2 assists and 2 blocks in 43 minutes of play. There was speculation that the 1997–98 season would be the last time in Chicago for the trio of Pippen, Jordan, and Jackson. The Bulls followed up by playing against the Jazz once again in the 1998 NBA Finals to win their second three-peat.

After being a Bull for 11 eventful seasons, Pippen, the second all-time leader in points, assists, and steals behind Jordan in Bulls franchise history, was traded to the Houston Rockets for the lockout-shortened season of 1998–99. This decision received much publicity, including his only solo cover of *Sports Illustrated*. He teamed with Hakeem Olajuwon and Charles Barkley, to try to win a third championship for the Rockets, but the chemistry just was not there, especially with Barkley. The previous season, the Rockets with

Hakeem Olajuwon, Charles Barkley and Clyde Drexler only finished 41-41. Drexler retired after that disappointing campaign. Pippen was brought in for his championship quality play as well as for his leadership skills.

While Pippen's offensive production slipped to 14.5 points per game, his 6.5 points rebounding and 5.9 points assisting were as good as it had ever been. With a lockout shortened season, the Rockets tied the Lakers with a 31-19 record, but due to a tie-breaker, they ended up behind the Lakers for fifth place in the Western Conference. The Lakers would also go on to easily defeat the Rockets 3-1 in the first round of the playoffs. The lack of chemistry between the three superstars was really taking its toll, and Pippen may have never felt truly comfortable in the Houston offense revolving around Olajuwon and Barkley. Further sealing the doomed fate, Pippen and Barkley's personal relationship also crumbled. What was once camaraderie became disdain between the two. In the off-season, the two exchanged harsh words through the media and Pippen after just one season in Houston was then traded to the Portland Trail Blazers.

Pippen spent the next four seasons with Portland, with the team's best season coming in his first year. He was the leader of the team that finished 59-12, and also finished second best in the league behind Pacific Division champs the Los Angeles Lakers. The two teams would also meet for a showdown in the Western Conference Finals. After going down 3-1, the Trail Blazers miraculously forced a Game 7 and upon entering the fourth quarter, they had amassed a 15 point lead. However, an improbable comeback by the Lakers sent them to the Finals where they eventually won the NBA title. Some people say that if the Blazers had managed to get past L.A., Pippen could have potentially won a championship there and cemented his legacy. The Blazers would make a postseason run in each of the next three seasons that Pippen was in a Portland uniform, but an assortment of injuries significantly reduce the amount of time he spent on the court. Although, in his last season in Portland, he still managed to be a key player even as he aged.

In his final NBA season, Pippen would return to the city of Chicago, where the Bulls had languished near the bottom of the Eastern Conference since the dynasty he led with Jordan in the 90s broke up. He would only play in 23 games, but the most valuable things he brought to the team were experience, veteran leadership, and mentoring a corps of young players that would help the team return to the playoffs the following year for the first time since 1997-98.

Pippen was a constant presence in the NBA Playoffs during his amazing career, reaching the playoffs for 16 straight years (11 with Chicago, 1 with Houston, 4 with Portland), and he even still holds the record for most steals in the Playoffs.

Chapter 4: Pippen's Personal Life

In 2010, Pippen traded in the brutally cold winters in Chicago for a warm tropical setting. He resides in south Florida. In 2005 and 2006, he began his work as a studio analyst in television broadcasts. He has also been in many advertisements since he began his lengthy NBA career, and has sometimes portrayed himself in guest appearances on television programs, including an appearance on *ER* in 1996. Pippen also has played three games for European basketball teams in 2008 for charity and has since served as an ambassador for the NBA overseas. On January 20, 2010, in a celebration fit for any basketball king, Pippen had his jersey retired by UCA.

Pippen has been married twice. The first marriage was short and was to Karen McCollum from 1988 to 1990. He married his second wife, Larsa in1997 and the two have been married since. He is also the father of five children. Pippen's children may have been the biggest influence behind his book, an autobiography geared towards children called *Reach Higher*, which was published in 1996. Although he is no longer in Chicago, Pippen continues to support various charities and causes across the city. Pippen has hosted many charity basketball games to support various causes, including tutoring programs for urban youth. He endorsed the 2012 Bank of America Chicago Marathon's special initiative, which showed support for US troops. Because Pippen's own father was a military man, the cause held a significant place in his heart. He and his wife came out to support the Bulls' franchise annual, "Evening with the Chicago Bulls" charity event in 2013. The fundraiser serves underprivileged residents of Chicago, and Pippen has revealed he considers it an honor to be able to give back to the city which had embraced him and shown him so much love and support. The couple also feel it is important for their children to see them involved in causes such as these because it allows them to set a good example of how to give back to the community.

In addition to all his NBA success, He has also represented the country at the senior levels and won gold medals in the 1992 and 1996 Summer Olympics on the United States basketball teams after a change in the rules allowed professional athletes to participate. In 2010, just 6 years after his retirement, he was inducted into the Naismith Memorial Basketball Hall of Fame. Two years later, he was named senior advisor to the Chicago Bulls' president and chief operating officer.

During 2010, Pippen made a comment saying that his teammate, Michael Jordan was the greatest scorer of all time, while stating that Lebron James is the best player ever to play basketball. He received much criticism for these remarks, namely from the greatest scorer of all time, Kareem Abdul-Jabbar. In an outrage, he sent a letter addressed to Pippen signed: Kareem Abdul-Jabbar, the NBA's all-time leading scorer.

"You obviously never saw Wilt Chamberlain play who undoubtedly was the greatest scorer this game has ever known. When did MJ ever average 50.4 points per game plus 25.7 rebounds? (Wilt in the 1962 season when blocked shot statistics were not kept). We will never accurately know how many shots Wilt blocked. Oh, by the way in 1967 and 68, Wilt was a league leader in assists. Did MJ ever score 100 points in a game? How many times did MJ score more than 60 points in a game? MJ led the league in scoring in consecutive seasons for 10 years but he did this in an NBA that eventually expanded into 30 teams vs. when Wilt played and there were only 8 teams."

-Dwyer, Kelly. "Kareem Abdul-Jabbar's nasty open letter to Scottie Pippen." ca.sports.yahoo.com N.p., 29 June 2010. Sunday, September 14, 2014.

After rattling off all of his impressive statistics, he then advised Pippen, "Do your research before giving anyone a number one title."

Chapter 5: Impact on Basketball

When people discuss Pippen's career and the legacy he left during his 17 NBA seasons, it's impossible not to mention his teammate, Michael Jordan. Sure, while Pippen did play Robin to Jordan's Batman, the question to ask is who wouldn't? People that actually believe Pippen's hall of fame career was only because of the fact that he ran with Michael is ludicrous. The truth is that Pippen would have been a hall of famer for any team, any system, any coach, in any era 100% of the time. He was one of the league's greatest treasures at that time. Even if you look at the history of the NBA, Pippen's versatility was matched by few players, if any at all. Scottie Pippen was just simply an incredibly unique player. On defense, he utilized his freakishly unusual length along with strength, basketball IQ, and athleticism. There wasn't an area defensively that he couldn't excel in; it was just simply impossible. He was a lock-down defender capable of guarding three different positions; small forward, shooting guard and point guard. Remember when Phil Jackson would use Pippen to defend the other team's point guard, their opponents would not start their offense until there was 11 seconds left on the shot clock as Pippen would simply pressure the point guard right from the inbound. During his era and possibly beyond, he was the best perimeter and wing defender in the sport. Even today, the closest person to do what he did may be Lebron James, the best basketball player in the world right now. When he was forced to defend the low block, he easily succeeded there, too. He was truly a defensive mastermind with all the right tools.

For as versatile as he was on the defensive end, you could argue that he was even more versatile on offense. Pippen was basically the point guard for six of the Bulls championship teams; running the patented Triangle Offense. Certainly during crunch time, it was always Pippen crossing the half court mark to begin facilitating the Bulls' offense more often than any other player on that team. It seemed like he was always playing point guard, yet he was also an elite small forward. In NBA history, no other forward has more career assists than Pippen. He could also score off the dribble and was nearly impossible for opponents to defend. It was tough for opposing small forwards to defend him because he was often playing point guard. Yet, you couldn't defend him with a point guard; they were just too small. He was also a decent outside threat, 32% from downtown, and an above average free throw shooter compared to other NBA players during his time.

The truth of the matter is Batman would still be a crime fighting hero in Gotham without Robin and Sherlock Holmes would still solve crime mysteries without Watson. So, it seems only plausible that Jordan would still be the best player of all time with or without Pippen. He would still have championships, but would he have won six championship rings? Hence, Jordan would have needed a Pippen possibly more so than Pippen needed Jordan. Another important fact is that, when Jordan bolted the NBA in 1993 to pursue a baseball career, Pippen became the Bulls' unquestionable best player and could have possibly won the league's MVP award during that season. Without Jordan, The Pippen-led Bulls still managed to win 55 games (2 less than the previous season), took the Knicks to seven games in the Eastern Conference semi-finals and Pippen was either first or second in every major team statistic (points, rebounds, assists, steals, blocks). He was named MVP of the All-Star game. He proved he could lead a team and still be one of the league's best players. Pippen could easily have been the Lone Ranger, Sherlock Holmes or even Batman on just about any other team. Pippen played basketball the way it was intended to be played. He was selfless as a teammate, he was an athletic rarity, and he was willing to play hard on both ends of the court. He had arrogance like the superstar that he was, and yet he exuberated humility and he carried himself with dignity. At times he could easily take over the game, dominating teammates and opponents with long scoring stretches or timely defensive actions such as astounding passes or dubiously sneaking the ball out of the opponents' hands. Many may not be familiar with Pippen's skills and history as quite possibly one of the greatest lockdown perimeter defenders in basketball. His 10 NBA All-Defensive honors and 8 NBA All-Defensive First Team awards are each one shy of the all-time record. He does hold the all-time NBA record for most assists and steals from the forward position, which Pippen basically revolutionized as well.

Again, this is not about a "who was better" competition between Pippen and Jordan. It is about realizing Pippen's efforts and impact in the world of basketball, and respecting it. The fact of the matter is that both of their skill level was closer than one would think. Granted, Jordan was and is the eternal recognizable face of sports across the globe, but every superhero has a sidekick and those sidekicks establish a reputation and following all their own. No player can win championships alone, and certainly not six of them, not even your royal "high"ness, Michael Jordan.

To sum it up, when Jordan was dropping 50 points some nights, Pippen was holding the opponent's best player under 20 points easily. He would also frequently carry the stretches when Jordan would rest and lead the second unit for the Bulls. Pippen's game just complimented the team so perfectly. He was highly competitive and was willing to do one thing that separates him from most players, being willing to sacrifice his stats to win championships. Still, somehow he always manages to get lost in the discussions of great players in NBA history, a place where he should always be relevant.

Chapter 6: Most Memorable Moments

Scottie Pippen wasn't just a mere sidekick to Michael Jordan; he had plenty of clutch moments himself. He possesses a certain magic many players just do not have. This magic is killer instinct. He has a proven history of making big shots when everything is on the line.

While it's obvious that Jordan is at least one of the greatest players ever, and one of the most clutch players ever, there were instances where Pippen did it all, and was easily the best player on the court. While Pippen may appear to have a lack of incredibly memorable shots compared to Jordan, it was Pippen who always set Jordan up, giving him the opportunities for those shots to happen.

1993 Eastern Conference Finals, Game 6

Closing out Game 5 in an unbelievable manner, the Bulls then returned to their home court for a pivotal Game 6. This was a must win game for the Bulls as the

Knicks were unbelievably good at Madison Square Garden. The Bulls managed to secure their third championship in 3 years with a 96-88 victory over the New York Knicks. It was Pippen who was clearly the best player on the floor that series, and time after time, bailing out the Bulls with consecutive big shots. Pippen played incredibly well that game finishing with 24 points, 6 assists, and 7 rebounds on a 50% Field Goal percentage.

During the game, and with only three and a half minutes left to go in the game, Pippen barely managed to get off a shot in time to avoid turning the ball over. This then gave the Bulls an 85-80 lead, which then gave the Bulls the momentum in the remaining minutes in the game. Once again, with a minute left, Pippen sealed the game with a 3-pointer to effectively end the series.

1993 Eastern Conference Finals, Game 4

In Game 4 of that same series against the Knicks, and with the Bulls attempting to even the series, it was once again up to Pippen to hit the clutch shot. With an isolation play set up for him, Pippen used his speed and then drove to the right. Unable to handle Pippen, the player had to foul him and give him the bucket and the free throw. This play gave the Bulls the lead at 97-90 with only a mere two minutes left.

1998 Eastern Conference Finals, Game 7

First, it was stirring just to go back and watch the fourth quarter of this game, in which the Bulls beat the Pacers 88-83 on sheer core and will. Chicago played with so much heart in this one, in front of an excited and anxious United Center crowd. The Bulls had a 22-4 edge in offensive rebounds, with Jordan and Pippen leading the way, combining for 11 O-boards.

Again, it was Pippen who made the game's decisive shots. As the reporter reported, "Pippen also made two big shots down the stretch and the Bulls held the Pacers scoreless over the final 2:05 as they reached the Finals for the sixth time in eight years." The first of the two shots gave Chicago an 81-79 lead with four minutes and forty seconds left, and came after Pippen fought past Reggie Miller for the offensive rebound.

Then, with two minutes to go, Pippen converted this tough runner while being fouled, extending Chicago's lead to 87-83. A last second free throw would be the only other scoring, and the Bulls were on their way to the 1998 Finals.

1991 Finals, Game 5

Pippen posts a 32-13-7 with 5 steals in the game which clinches Chicago's first championship.

1992 Eastern Conference Finals, Game 6

In a game that has been on an endless loop on NBA TV in recent days, Pippen displayed his all-around brilliance with a 29-12-5, plus 4 blocks and 4 steals, as the Bulls beat the Cavs to win the series.

1992 Finals, Game 6

Facing a 15-point deficit going into the fourth quarter of Game Six of the 1992 NBA Finals versus the Portland Trail Blazers, Pippen led the Bulls' reserves on a 14-2 run before Michael Jordan and the remaining starters re-joined him on the floor to seal the team's second NBA Championship.

Chicago's 33-14 domination in the final frame was just enough for the Bulls to secure the 97-93 victory. The star of the miraculous rally, Pippen, finished the game with 26 points (9 of 17 shooting, 6 of 9 from the line), five rebounds and four boards.

1998 Eastern Conference Finals, Game 1

Scoring only four points, Scottie Pippen dominated Game One of the Eastern Conference finals against Indiana with his defense on Pacers point guard Mark

Jackson, who turned the ball over seven times in an 85-79 Bulls victory. Pippen struggled from the field, but managed seven assists, grabbed seven boards and added four steals in the win.

Pippen shot 1 for 9 and scored four points and totally dominated the game. That is what makes him one of the greatest players ever. He does not have to score a point and he can control the whole game. Scottie Pippen had heart, he had toughness, and he delivered in big games and big moments over and over and over again.

Chapter 7: Pippen's Legacy and Future

One of the most versatile and talented players ever, Scottie Pippen orchestrated the offense like a point guard, rebounded like a power forward, scored like a shooting guard and defended on the perimeter like few others in NBA history. The seven-time All-Star was a vital component to the Chicago Bulls' six NBA championships runs in the 1990s. In 17 seasons, Pippen missed the postseason only in his final campaign, allowing him to rack up the second most playoff appearances (208) ever, behind only the great Kareem Abdul-Jabbar (237). More than anything though, his all-around game became the prototype for the next generation of small forwards, like the players you see today. As the side-kick, the second-best player on the championship Bulls teams alongside Michael Jordan, there is a high possibility Pippen may never get his respect. The question you have to ask is how much of Pippen's success was a result of his association with Jordan. His achievements speak volumes.

Pippen was a member of the 50th Anniversary Team, a two-time gold medal Olympian with the Dream Team in 1992 and in 1996, and became the first player to win the NBA championship and an Olympic gold twice. He also made a fair amount of appearances on the All-NBA defensive teams, eight times to be exact (1992-1999), as well as the 1994 NBA All-Star MVP; not an easy feat for anyone. Yet, his career averages of 16.1 points per game, 6.4 rebounds and 5.2 assists were not staggering like Jordan's, but Pippen was a different type of player. This quote sums it up perfectly, "Pippen was the ultimate supporting player, the perfect complement."

Scottie Pippen was an extraordinary offensive player; playing with one of the biggest ball-dominating players of all time Michael Jordan. Still, he scored 20 points a game, not just by making cuts or knocking down open shots, but by using his ball handling and athleticism to drive to the hole and finish resoundingly. He scored with his back to the basket using his height, wingspan, and a huge collection of post moves he acquired over the years, and a deadly shot to boot. He could also hit open jumpers and move without the ball for easy scores. Thinking that Pippen simply took advantage of the opportunities given to him by Jordan is vastly underestimating his true existence as an offensive player. His chief role on offense wasn't even to be a scorer. It was to be a true point forward, whose court vision, passing (he averaged 6 or 7 assists per game during each of the Bulls legendary championship years), and understanding of the offense was crucial to working the legendary triangle offense that won the Chicago Bulls all of those championships.

Of course, there was his defense. Arguably, he was the best defensive player on one of the best defensive teams of all time. He was most likely the best perimeter defender of all time; it was always Pippen who got to shut down the other team's best scorer, and not Jordan. It was also Pippen known for rotating over to provide the best defensive help of just about anybody. He regularly made more steals than anyone in the league even to this date, and made enough blocks to put him on par with most career centers. Scottie Pippen is without a doubt, simply one of the greatest players to have graced the game of basketball.

Final Word/About the Author

I was born and raised in Norwalk, Connecticut. Growing up, I could often be found spending many nights watching basketball, soccer, and football matches with my father in the family living room. I love sports and everything that sports can embody. I believe that sports are one of most genuine forms of competition, heart, and determination. I write my works to learn more about influential athletes in the hopes that from my writing, you the reader can walk away inspired to put in an equal if not greater amount of hard work and perseverance to pursue your goals. If you enjoyed *Scottie Pippen: The Inspiring Story of One of Basketball's Greatest Small Forwards* please leave a review! Also, you can read more of my works on *Kobe Bryant, Carmelo Anthony, Kevin Love, Grant Hill, Tracy McGrady, Vince Carter, Patrick Ewing, Karl Malone, Tony Parker, Allen Iverson, Hakeem Olajuwon, Reggie Miller, Michael Carter-Williams,*

John Wall, Stephen Curry, James Harden, Tim Duncan, and *Steve Nash* in the Kindle Store.

Made in the USA
Middletown, DE
04 September 2015